PROSPER

Live with Generosity,
Live in Blessing

by
Steve Kelly

Table of Contents

Introduction

Over the past fifty years, there have been hundreds, if not thousands, of Christian books written about prosperity.

Many of those books are based on sound teaching and understanding of God's principles. For example, sowing and reaping is a natural and spiritual truth. God's plan is to bless His people, not to harm them.[1] Jesus did say that whoever follows Him would reap "now in the present age, houses, brothers and sisters..."[2]

The aim of this book is not to refute or really even add to the work of many books that have taught the true values of God's design for His people to have and receive financial blessing.

This book is broader than finances. Finances are important, to be sure, but life is more than money.

---

[1] Jeremiah 29:11
[2] Mark 10:30 (NIV)

Jesus said, "Isn't life more than food and the body more than clothing?"[3] He taught us to think about more than material things.

Just before that, in Matthew 6:24 (NIV), He said, "No man can serve two masters...You cannot serve God and money."

Too often, we fall into the trap of believing that money is the proof of God's favor. Because it's at the center of our interaction with the things we need to live and function in modern society, money becomes the tool and the gauge for determining how blessed we are. But life is more than a "give to get" plan. Life is more than budgets and spreadsheets and 401Ks, though all those things are necessary.

Life is not what we possess. Life is what we pass on to others. Life is not just building a financial inheritance for your children; it's modeling an abundant heart of gratitude that infects everyone around you.

---

[3] Matthew 6:25 (NIV)

I chose the title for this book very strategically. You see; a prosperous life is a generous life. A generous life is a blessed life. Regardless of material accumulation, the Bible promises that the "generous person will prosper, and whoever refreshes others will be refreshed."[4]

To prosper means to have abundance in many areas. Physical health. Spiritual peace. Marital bliss. Joyful children. A great reputation. The list could go on and on. You get the point. Being blessed is about what you have left over *after* you've paid your bills.

Prospering is not about buying things you can't afford to impress others. In fact, Solomon, who had more material wealth than anyone in history warned, "it's better to have a sleeping dog than a dead lion."[5] He meant that it was better to have something effective and useful but less impressive on the surface than to have a majestic creature

---

[4] Proverbs 11:25 (NIV)
[5] Ecclesiastes 9:4 (NIV)

that has no power because it's dead. It's no benefit to have a superficially impressive possession if it was paid for by getting a huge debt you can't afford. It's better to have a less significant house or car that you can afford, than to carry the crushing burden of debt and live under stress and worry.

Too often, instead of thanking God we have a roof over our head (which billions of people don't), we only pray for a *bigger* roof over our head.

My true prayer is that you would prosper. But, as John writes, "I pray that you prosper in all things and be in health, just as your soul prospers."[6]

---

[6] 3 John 1:2

So, that's my prayer as well. I pray that as you read this book, you understand the full meaning of a prosperous life. I pray that you comprehend the breadth and depth of God's desire for your life. A life meant to be lived without needless anxiety and worry about tomorrow. A life that is generous, and therefore blessed. I pray that you prosper.

Sincerely,
Steve Kelly

Responsibility

Recently, a television commercial for auto insurance has promoted the "safe driver discount". This discount provides a reduction in premium costs for someone who drives accident-free for a period of time. Of course, this is a benefit for the insurance company as well, since the company won't have to pay any money out for drivers who have no accidents.

Not to be outdone, another major insurance provider has a commercial that promotes the benefit to the general community when everyone takes responsibility for helping others. Similarly, this inspiration is meant to reduce the costs that the insurance company has to bear. If people are more responsible, they will avoid dangerous situations or risky endeavors that lead to increased accidents and damage.

The part that caught my attention was the slogan at the end of the commercial. A rich baritone voice comes on at the conclusion and says, "Responsibility: What's Your Policy?"

This message struck me as direct and clear, but also as a bit unusual in modern media. I'm used to hearing slogans like "You deserve a break today" or "Have it your way". These messages promote self-indulgence. They promote products that bring temporary happiness or at least satisfy hunger. But they are opposite of the responsibility slogan.

About 3,000 years ago, King Solomon wrote, "there is nothing new under the sun."[7]

The responsibility message is just another bit of evidence to reinforce Solomon's truth. Long before television was invented, long before mutual insurance companies existed in the United States of America; long before the USA existed, God declared the importance of responsibility.

---

[7] Ecclesiastes 1:9 (NIV)

In fact, responsibility has been one of God's policies since the beginning of creation, when he told Adam and Eve to be responsible for their actions. When they failed to exercise responsible self-control, the collateral damage caused God to set into motion the greatest insurance policy ever.

He sent His son Jesus to save us all from the effect of sin, and Jesus took responsibility for all of us on the cross.

How does this connect to a prosperous life? It does, and more than we realize; or at least consciously recognize.
You see, God tells us early on that we are responsible for our decisions. Every decision has a consequence. The accumulation of consequences yields a life that is either prosperous or deficient.

Until we admit that we are responsible for our decisions, we will remain delusional and disillusioned. We will blame others for our circumstances and for the absence of blessing in our lives.

God told the Israelites in Exodus 19:5, "If you obey Me fully and keep my covenant, then out of all the nations, you will be my treasured possession."

God wants to bless and honor His people. He adores us. His promises are unbreakable. The limitations on His ability to grant us a prosperous life are only imposed by our unwillingness to obey Him fully.

I used the word "unwillingness" intentionally. The truth is, I could have used the word "inability" and I would have been just as accurate. We are unable of fully obeying His commands. But, He is less concerned about our inability than our availability. Are we willing? Are we submitted? Jesus died and God sent His Holy Spirit to empower us.

His strength is made perfect in our weakness.[8]

He will enable us. But He will not force us to do anything we are unwilling to do. In fact, if a person

---

[8] 2 Corinthians 12:9

continually resists God, He will eventually stop trying to rescue him.[9]

Remain willing. Remain obedient. One of God's main promises to His people, and to us all Christians as heirs to His promise, is found in Isaiah 1:19-20 (NIV): "If you are willing and obedient, you will eat the good things of the land." Serving God is the key to blessing. Willing obedience honors Him and makes Him desire to bless you more.

One of the key ways to do this is to take responsibility. Take responsibility for your thoughts, your words, and your actions.

The beginning of true prosperity is found when we admit from our innermost being that we need Jesus. When we take responsibility for our failures by placing them at His feet. The beginning of the blessed life is when we stop blaming others, and start blessing them with words of encouragement and affirmation. We can only do this when we

---

[9] Romans 1:28

accept responsibility and admit that God's ways are true and righteous altogether.

In his second inaugural address, Abraham Lincoln quoted Psalm 19:9, as I did in the previous sentence. "The judgments of the Lord are true and righteous altogether."

This is a powerful expression of God's majesty. He doesn't make mistakes. His decisions and His commands are righteous. When we take responsibility for our lives and begin to align our behavior with His standards, we initiate the steps that lead to a prosperous life.

One of my favorite verses is "How good and pleasant it is when God's people live in unity...there the Lord commands His blessing, even life forevermore."[10]

If God commands His blessing when people are in unity, how much more will He pour out His blessing when we live in unity with His commands? I

---

[10] Psalm 133:1-3

encourage you to think deeply about responsibility. What does it mean to accept your situation and take ownership? What does it mean to admit to God that you fall short? What does it mean to accept His forgiveness and commit to follow His will? Taking responsibility is not easy, but if you want to life a prosperous life, it's necessary.

Choose Life

"Some choices we live not only once but a thousand times over, remembering them for the rest of our lives." – Richard Bach

I share this quote not to trouble you, nor to discourage you. I share it to remind you that our choices have consequences. I share it as a reminder of the man's limited perspective. Man is naturally predisposed to rehearse his choices. But God tells us that "there is now no condemnation for those who are in Christ Jesus."[11]

Regardless of your choices so far in life, God can forgive the bad ones and He can build on the good ones. Today is a new day, with new opportunities for better decisions. For Godly decisions.

The amazing thing is, He lets us decide. I believe He gave us the ability to decide and it's up to us to make the choice to prosper. I believe prosperity is

---

[11] Romans 8:1 (NIV)

not a preference. It's not happenstance. It's not fate or good fortune. It's a conviction. It's a firm decision that prospering is our calling as Christians, and that's because prosperity isn't just for us. We are to prosper so that we can help and bless others.

Thousands of years ago, He spelled out the opportunity He gave us to choose. The following passage is found in Deuteronomy 30:10-20. The entire passage is included here because it's worth the read. It provides a clear contrast between choosing between life and death. Make no mistake – our choices are leading us in one direction or the other. As He begs the Israelites, He's pleading with us today: Choose Life:

> *If you obey the voice of the Lord your God, to keep His commandments...which are written in this Book of the Law, and if you turn to the Lord your God with all your heart and with all your soul.*

For this commandment which I command you today is not too hard for you, nor is it far off.

It is not in heaven, that you should say, "Who will ascend into heaven for us and bring it to us, that we may hear it and do it?"

Nor is it beyond the sea, that you should say, "Who will go over the sea for us and bring it to us, that we may hear it and do it?"

But the word is very near you, in your mouth and in your heart, that you may do it.

See, I have set before you today, life and good, death and evil, in that I command you today to love the Lord your God, to walk in His ways, and to keep His commandments

*...**that you may live and multiply (<u>prosper</u>);** and the Lord your God will bless you in the land which you go to possess.*
***But if your heart turns away** so that you do not hear, and are drawn away, and worship other gods and serve them,*

I announce to you today that you will surely perish; you will not prolong your days in the land which you cross over the Jordan to go in and possess.

*I call heaven and earth as witnesses today against you, **that I have set before you life and death, blessing and cursing; therefore choose life, that both you and your descendants may live;** that you may love the Lord your God, that you may obey His voice and that you may cling to Him,*

For He is your life and the length of your days...

This passage is a beautifully written explanation of God's order. He gives His people the choice between life and death, then tells them how much He longs for them to choose life. Finally, He tells them that *He is their life*, if only they will choose Him.

This section of the Old Testament explains not only the consequences of the choice, but also how to locate it, define it, and decide it.

1. **It's not too hard.** Verse 11 explains that the choice is not too difficult. It's not impossible. Many times, I've counseled people who claim that the decision they are facing is too hard. The reality is they are not yet making their decision based on God's order. Whatever choices you face today, there is one that leads to life. It may be emotionally taxing, it may be physically overwhelming, but it is not too hard. Trust God. Listen to the Holy Spirit. Choose the decision that leads to life.

2. **It's not all on God.** Verse 12 tells us that "it's not in heaven." Too many times I have watched people who don't take action because they are waiting for God to confirm something they are doing. I believe we waste time and miss opportunities when we "wait on God". I think He's waiting on us! Ecclesiastes 9:10 offers wisdom on this – "Whatever your hand finds to do, do it with all your might…" Sometimes, we need to stop looking up and start looking at what's in front of us and go to work!

In Exodus 14:15-31, the Israelites demonstrate (once again) the tendency we all have to moan and cry when things don't look good. They had just been rescued from Egypt and were standing in front of the Red Sea. The Egyptian army was gaining on them, and Moses was trying to keep them calm. As he prayed, God replied, "Why are you crying out to me? Tell the Israelites to move on. Raise your staff and stretch out your hand over the sea to divide the water so that the Israelites can go through the sea on dry ground." (v. 15-16)

God told Moses, "Go! Move! Take action! Quit talking about it, quit praying about it. Get up and go!" It's not all up to God. It's sometimes up to us. Pick yourself up today and get started. Go for what you believe God wants you to do.

3. **It's not all the devil's fault.** Verse 13 tells us it's not in the depths of the sea. It's not in the center of the earth. It's not in the bowels of the world, where hell is typically thought to be. In Moses time, there was a punishment that happened where men were swallowed up by an earthquake. Too often, we think that the devil is the source of our

problems. The truth is most of our problems come from our own flesh.

I once visited a man in the hospital who needed a hip and knee replacement. He was very obese and the doctors told him he had to lose weight before he could have the surgery. When I went to pray with him, he asked me to rebuke the devil. I told him, "no problem, but we need to rebuke the knife and fork!" It wasn't the devil that caused him to overeat, it was his flesh.

I experience conversations like that all the time. Too many Christians are looking to blame the devil when they need to look in the mirror. It's all too common for people to think they need "deliverance". I think, most of the time, deliverance is just a cop out because they don't want to truly repent and get rid of their sins. Quit blaming the devil –

all the problems we have don't come from hell.

4. **It's near you. It's in your mouth. It's in your heart.** Verse 14 is the heart of the whole passage. It brings the point to conclusion and gives us the understanding that choosing life is possible. It's a matter of what's in our hearts; because as a man thinks in his heart, so is he.[12] If it's not easy for you to have thoughts that choose life, I encourage you to renew your mind.

It's a process but it's necessary. Your mind is renewed by what you focus on, and by making right choices. In my book, *Choose: Your Daily Decisions Determine Your Destiny*, I share the principles that will allow you to renew your mind. As you renew your mind, your speech will follow.

---

[12] Proverbs 23:7

The truth is, we do get to choose. Every day, in big and small ways, we are choosing either life or death. Choose Life.

A Friend of Jesus

"You are my friends, if you do what I command."[13] So said Jesus, while talking to his disciples about the nature of having an abiding relationship with Him. More accurately, *in Him*.

The story that comes before this verse is an analogy about the vine and its branches. Jesus told the disciples that He was the vine, and they were the branches. He explained that they had the choice to remain connected or not, but if they didn't remain connected, they would be unable to bear fruit. They would be cut off from the blessing that comes with being a friend of Jesus.

After reading this, some people might scratch their head and say, "But I thought Jesus was nice to everyone. Why would He make people obey Him to be His friend? How could he be so harsh?"

---

[13] John 15:14 (NIV)

It is true that Jesus came to Earth to do away with the Law; that long list of rules and duties and sacrifices that the people of Israel had to follow to try to stay in right relationship with God. It is true that Jesus showed mercy to people. It is true that Jesus made the only way to salvation when He died and rose again from the dead.

All that is true, and more, but the reality is ***though we live in a New Covenant, life with Jesus still requires order and structure.***
Fortunately for us, instead of thousands of difficult rules, the New Covenant brought two key principles. These principles are what Jesus asks of his disciples, and of you and me: *Love the Lord your God with all your heart and all your soul and all your strength and with all your mind, and love your neighbor as much as you love yourself.*[14]

If you obey these principles, you are obeying Jesus' commands. So you see, what may have initially seemed like a stern, overbearing directive is simply

---

[14] Luke 10:27 (NIV)

an explanation that abiding in Jesus requires alignment with His heart.

This is another opportunity to make the right decisions. If this book has a recurring theme, it's the understanding that our choices are steering us toward a prosperous life. Or not. Choosing to be a friend of Jesus is essential to live a life of generosity and blessing.

Sometimes, that choice will lead to difficult decisions. Sometimes, Jesus will ask us to do things – or stop doing things – that are not easy. Our flesh wants to do things that will ultimately bring harm and death to our life. Jesus wants to cut away that things that are choking our prosperity. I often say, "Not all growth is good. If you have a large tumor growing on your body, it needs to be removed." There are things in each of our lives that need to be removed so we can grow in a healthy, prosperous way.

It's like I tell my children, "I love you no matter what, but I want other people to like you too, so I discipline you."

God wants us to prosper and help others. Therefore, he disciplines us. Just before Jesus talked about obeying His commands, He talked about the reality that God prunes the branches in the vine that are bearing fruit. The pruning is disciplining the branch for greater growth.

In order to fully live prosperous, generous and blessed, we have to endure pruning. We have to obey His commands, and remain in Him. When we are truly a friend of Jesus, we will obey and discover the tremendous flourishing growth that He desires for our lives.

The connection between obedience and blessing isn't just something that Jesus discussed. From the beginning, God instilled in His people the consequences of disobedience, and the benefits of obedience. The prophet Isaiah told the Israelites, "If you are willing and obedient, you will eat the good things of the land."[15]

---

[15] Isaiah 1:19 (NIV)

God wants us to have the *best* of the land. But, His blessing is not a hand-out from heaven. It requires obedience. Many people want to "interpret" God's command for themselves by twisting the meaning of the words or fitting the instruction into their own pre-existing paradigm. There is no need for interpretation.

Like Moses, who presumed on God's command for the miracle of retrieving water from a rock, we sometimes do what God asks, but we do it our way. God told Moses to speak to the rock.[16] Did Moses obey? No. He let his anger with the complaining Israelites influence his actions. Instead of speaking to the rock, Moses hit the rock with his staff. There might not seem to be a big difference between speaking to the rock and smacking it. But, to God, it made all the difference in the world. Moses disobeyed. And in the verse right after he hits the rock, God told him, "Because you did not trust in Me enough to honor me as holy in the sight

---

[16] Numbers 20:8

of the Israelites, you will take them into the land (the Promised Land) that I have given."[17]

Moses did what worked the last time, instead of obeying God's "now" word. How often do we act in a similar manner? We tend to fall back on whatever worked in the past, instead of listening for God's new directions. We become overly familiar with God and keep him boxed into our old experiences with Him. Listen to Him. Don't automatically do things the way you've always done it. It could be that, like Moses, God wants you to do things a different way.

Moses didn't obey God and it cost him the fullness of God's blessing. Even though Moses disobeyed, the Israelites did get the water from the rock, but it was bitter. It was tainted and didn't taste good. Anytime we disobey God, we limit the fullness of what He desires to bring into our life. His intention was to refresh the Israelites. Because of Moses'

---

[17] Numbers 20:12

disobedience, they got the necessary, but they didn't get the abundant.

It's the same for you and me. When we disobey, we don't have the same connection to the fullness of God. We erode our friendship with Jesus. The lesson of Moses is for all of us. Obey Him directly and completely, and we will receive the refreshing we need for today, and we will be able to enter the entirety of His promise in the days to come.

Listen

As I mentioned, I often explained the need for discipline to my children. If you are a parent, you know what I mean. Sometimes it can seem like you spend all day telling your kids to pick up after themselves, to do their homework, or to help with the dishes.

The following is a typical experience for any parent:

> Dad: *Son, can you please take out the trash before you go to bed tonight?*
>
> Son: (ears covered in headphones) *Sure.*
>
> Dad: (the next morning) *Son, I thought I asked you to take out the trash last night? I just went out to the garage and it's still sitting there.*
>
> Son: *What?*

Dad: *I said, why didn't you take out the trash last night like I asked you?*

Son: *You did?*

Dad: *Yes, I did.*

Son: *Sorry, Dad, I guess I didn't hear you.*

If you are a parent, you are either grinning or grimacing at this fictional conversation. And if you are a son, don't worry, one day you'll have the same conversation with your son.

This example is familiar and even a little funny. The consequences of the son's failure to obey aren't very bad – unless it's a really hot week and you have garbage pile up until the next week's pick-up. It makes me wonder, though - How often God asks us to do something – maybe take out the trash that is piling up in our life? How often do we say "yes" but fail to follow through?

Or worse, how often are we walking around listening to distractions – like the son's headphones – and we don't even hear God?

We have to listen to God. And when He speaks, we need to obey. There is no way to live the generous and blessed life that leads to real prosperity without listening to God.

The New Covenant writer of the book of Hebrews repeats an Old Covenant[18] truth about the importance of listening.

"Today, *if you hear His voice*; if you don't harden your hearts…we will come to share (be a part of the blessing) in Christ."[19]

It is a compelling truth that hasn't changed with the coming of Jesus. There is a condition to our ability to join in with the blessings that come from relationship with God. That condition is our

---

[18] Psalm 95

[19] Hebrews 3:8, 14 (NIV)

hearing. We are not without consequence, even though we are in the New Covenant.

Similarly, forgiveness of sin is instantaneous but the consequences of sin remain. If we break the law, we can ask for forgiveness, but the judge will still put us in jail. We must listen to God. If we do, we will hear and can obey and find true prosperity.

Some people may read this section and feel frustrated because they want to obey. They just don't know how to hear from God. Hearing from God goes first. If we don't know how to hear, we won't know how to obey. Everyone can hear from God. Here are some ways to listen to His voice:

> **Personal Prayer.** One way to hear God's voice is in your own prayer. Make time to spend talking to Him as often as you can. Be by yourself. As you prayer, you will hear thoughts in your own voice. That's God speaking to you. When He speaks, Listen.

Read the Bible. The Bible is the written Word of God. But it's more than letters on a page. It's alive with the truth and power of God himself. As you read the Bible, you will begin to see how it applies to every situation in life. You will realize how no book on Earth can substitute for the inspired, powerful words of God. Read your Bible. Listen to it and obey.

Actively listen to the preaching of God's Word. In addition to reading the Bible and praying, you need to listen to men and women of God preach. And, you need more than just listening to podcasts of some preacher you've never met. You need to get involved in a local church that preaches the Bible and encourages you to bring God's Word to life.

You see, after you've heard, your faith will grow. How do I know? Not only have I experienced it firsthand many times in my life, but God's Word also tells us.

Romans 10:17 – "Consequently, faith comes by hearing the message, and the message is heard through the word of Christ."

As we hear more and more, our faith grows, which in turn, helps us be more obedient, which leads to a life that truly prospers. It's not only spiritually vital that we listen to the preaching of the Word, it's refreshing and inspiring. It fills you with the necessary faith to keep pursuing God with your whole heart. So, read the Bible, pray regularly, and get involved in church. Listen to God.

Repent

In the very early days of the New Testament church, a serious and scary story is told of two people who failed to repent. The choices of Ananias and Sapphira, husband and wife, and the consequences of those choices, are recorded in Acts 5:1-11.

Essentially, they conspired to deceive the apostles by telling them that the financial offering they were preparing to give was the total profit from the sale of property.

First, Ananias came into the church and gave the money, explaining (likely with great flourish) that the offering was the full profit. Peter was told by the Holy Spirit that Ananias was lying.

Peter asked Ananias why he would lie to God. And, then Ananias fell down dead.

That's right, Ananias died. Now, I don't know exactly why he died, but I think it's clear that deception about generosity is not a good idea.

Three hours later, Sapphira came in, still unaware of her husband's death. She was given the opportunity to repent and confess that she and her husband were attempting to deceive God.

Peter asked her, "Tell me, is this the price you and Ananias got for the land?"
"Yes," she said, "that is the price."

"How could you conspire to test the Spirit of the Lord," Peter said. "Listen! The feet of the men who buried your husband are at the door, and they will carry you out also."[20]

Sure enough, Sapphira fell down dead and was carried out to be buried with her husband.

I bring up this story not to frighten people. I bring it up because it gives a remarkable insight into the priority of God. He clearly values integrity, especially in the area of financial stewardship.

---

[20] Acts 5:7-9 (NIV)

Peter emphasized God's heart as well, when before Ananias died, Peter said, "The property was yours in the beginning, you didn't have to sell it. And, after you sold it, wasn't the money at your disposal? What made you thing of doing such a thing? You have not lied just to human beings but you have lied to God."[21]

There is a reason that financial integrity is tied to a prosperous life. There is a reason that Jesus talked about money more than He talked about Heaven and Hell combined. In fact, nearly one-third of the parables had to do with finances.

Our financial integrity should be high and it should reflect God's nature. We should honor Him, even in little ways. Years ago, I was on a family vacation with one of my relatives. We all had young children, and we went to a swimming pool that had a lot of fun slides and we were excited to splash and play with our kids. As we were paying our admission ticket, I heard my relative tell the

---

[21] Acts 5:3-4 (NIV)

attendant that all her kids were under age 10. I knew this wasn't true, and I wondered why. When it came my turn to pay, I realized why. The ticket was a couple dollars cheaper for children under 10.

I paid full price for my children, and asked my relative why she would lie to save a couple dollars. She shrugged it off, but all I could think was how sad. The price of her integrity was saving a couple dollars at a vacation spot. The truth is, integrity is revealed most in the little things, when no one is watching.

At Wave Church, I've had the opportunity to hire people who I felt were called by God and could have been great for the work. But, when reviewing their records, I discovered they weren't tithing. They didn't get the job. If a seasoned Christian isn't tithing, they won't get the job. That's a lack of integrity. God must be first in our finances. Now, if it's a new Christian who came to me for help and was working on tithing, that would be a different matter. But, if a person knows better, they should be better. God wants us to have a proper and healthy relationship with money. He wants our hearts to be fully after Him, not money. Just before Ananias and Sapphira, in Acts 4:36-37, mention is made of a man named Joseph, who was renamed Barnabas. He sold a field and brought all the money into the church. I think Ananias and Sapphira wanted to be like Barnabas. They just didn't want to make the sacrifice. Instead, they lied when they didn't have to, and ended up dead.

Now, to the point of this section – **Repentance**.

Sapphira was given a chance to repent. Peter asked her directly if the offering was truly the full sale price of the property. In that moment, I believe she could have admitted the truth and her life would have been spared. Who knows? Perhaps the rest of her life would have continued to be blessed. After all, she and Ananias must have been somewhat affluent, as they could afford to sell property and give a large sum of money to the church.

If only she'd repented.

Blessing comes from having a repentant heart. God wants us to be zealous to repent. That means we should be quick to ask forgiveness as soon as we know we've been disobedient. And, it's key to remember that apologizing because we get caught is not the same thing as repenting because we understand we are grieving the Holy Spirit.

I've had plenty of people cry crocodile tears after they were caught and the consequences of their action was severe and painful. Our desire should be to repent quickly. Our motivation should be to do what's right, always.

I heard about a pastor who was asked by a woman to have an affair. He told her no, which was good. But when she asked why, he told her he couldn't do it because he'd "lose his ministry." Not because he was married, or because God has standards for our behavior and it would be a sin. He had the right action in this case, but his motivation was sure wrong.

This principle is emphasized in the Old Testament and the New Testament. Let's take a look at 2 Corinthians 7 and 2 Chronicles 7:

"Godly sorrow leads to repentance that leads to salvation and leaves no regret, but worldly sorrow brings death."[22]

"If my people, who are called by my name, will humble themselves and pray and seek my face, and turn from their wicked ways, then I will hear from heaven and I will forgive their sin, and will heal their land."[23]

Repentance shows that you have the right heart posture before God. It unlocks His blessing. It leaves no regret. As He tells the Israelites in 2 Chronicles, if we repent, He will forgive and heal the land.
Healing the land has to do with the natural prosperity of fertile soil. Society was agrarian, and

---

[22] 2 Corinthians 7:10
[23] 2 Chronicles 7:14

therefore much of the wealth was found in the crops that were cultivated and grew in the ground. Livestock were dependent upon it. The people literally couldn't live unhealthy land. It's no different today, we just don't have as many farmers as they did back then.

And the principle is the same today. Repentance allows God to forgive and heal your land. Maybe your "land" is a business venture that went south. Maybe it's a relationship that used to produce great abundance, but something happened and a grudge created a rift. Whatever it might be, study your heart and see if there is a need to repent.

It might just be that a lack of repentance is keeping your "land" from being made whole. It might just be repentance that unlocks the work of God and brings true prosperity to your life!

Endure

Responsibility. Obedience. Repentance. Maybe
some of you are thinking, "this book sure is asking
a lot of me!"

Trust me. If it were easy, everyone would have a
prosperous life. Everyone would be living "the
good life", with plenty to spare and plenty to share.
There's a reason this book is titled *Prosper,* instead
of Prosperity. We often emphasize the material
gains of prosperity to the exclusion of the character
development that is required to truly *Prosper.*

My desire isn't to teach you how to make a lot of
money, although I believe God would love for you
to. My aim isn't to show you steps to financial
freedom, though I know God wants us all to be
great stewards.

My genuine prayer as I write this book is for you to
truly prosper. For your whole person, body, soul,
spirit, and mind to be fully complete, and ready to
do good work for the Lord. True prosperity isn't

found in the size of your bank account or the number of cars in your garage. True prosperity is found in giving your life, your time and your talents to be used by God in the service of others. Through the development of the character needed to do those things, you begin to truly prosper!

The final section of this book will give some detail for God's principles for financial management. But, I want to make sure you've grasped the deeper things first. Before you can grow in financial abundance, God wants you to be responsible, obedient, and repentant. And sometimes, even while doing all those things, you still might not see the blessing of God right away.

That's where the final character trait comes in. **Endurance.**

The single best Scripture for this point is found in Galatians. Paul wrote the letter that became the book of Galatians; he wrote it to a group of people who are described as "fierce warriors, who were respected by the Greeks and Romans. They were often hired as mercenary soldiers..."[24]

It's interesting that Paul's audience for the message on endurance was one that had a legacy of warfare. Naturally, if a group is notable for working as mercenaries, it's reasonable to assume that they possessed character traits like fortitude, determination, mental toughness – the things we admire about soldiers today.

In Galatians 6:9, Paul writes a very strong explanation of the need for endurance, to an audience that likely needed no reminder. If they needed that trait reinforced, it's clear that we do as well.

"Do not grow weary while doing good. For in due season, you will reap, if you don't faint."

---

[24] David Rankin, (1987) 1996. *Celts and the Classical World* (London: Routledge): Chapter 9 "The Galatians".

I tell people all the time, "don't bring your theology down to the level of your experiences." By that, I mean that sometimes in life we need to just keep believing. Sometimes we don't see what we believe should be happening or it feels like everything is crashing down around us. It's then that we need to listen to the words of Paul. It's then that we must endure.

Sometimes people in a tough position will ask, "How long do I have to trust God?"

My answer? "Until you're dead!"

I don't say that to be cheeky or disrespectful. I genuinely believe that there are times when all we can do is keep believing.

As the verse says, (1) don't grow weary, (2) in due season you'll reap, (3) if you don't faint.

Paul uses three different phrases to say the same thing – **Endure**.

He is encouraging the warrior spirit of the Galatians to keep fighting, keep believing, keep doing good. Likewise, we should be encouraged to endure. Don't walk away from your harvest. Hang in there. Fight the good fight.

Many times God allows us to endure because He knows it's preparing us for the next level of leadership He has planned. Just as farmers wait for their harvest, just as soldiers hold out during extreme conditions, we must endure to reap.

If we want to **Prosper**, We must **Endure.**

Give

OK. You've taken responsibility. You've been obedient. You've repented. You've endured.

I can hear you saying, "But, Pastor Steve, I want my harvest! I understand the need for character development and repentance and endurance. But, I still want the blessing that God has promised me!"

I understand. And you're right. God does want you to be blessed, in this life, and in the life to come.[25]

In my life, the foundational principle that has brought a prosperous life is being generous. Generosity is an essential necessity for prosperity. When you live with generosity, you live in blessing.

The first place to begin your generosity is in your giving to God. If you are not tithing, or never have, begin there. The tithe is 10% of your income. It is established by God as the method for supporting

---

[25] Luke 18:30

the work of the church and the salary for the pastors.

In Matthew 23:23, Jesus endorses tithing. He said, "Woe to you, scribes and Pharisees, hypocrites! For you pay tithe...and have omitted the weightier matters of the law, judgment, mercy, and faith: you should have practiced the latter, **without neglecting the former**."

In the Old Testament, Abraham tithed to Melchizedek.[26] Tithing existed during the Old Testament, through the Cross to the New Testament.

Jesus is telling the Pharisees to "grow up." They should tithe, of course, but they need to move beyond that. Tithing is basic. It's fundamental to establishing the right heart before God. Remember the section on becoming a friend of Jesus? Remember obedience? Tithing is simple obedience.

---

[26] Genesis 14:20

Since we're on the topic, I'll take this opportunity to illuminate an area of frequent confusion. That is, where does the tithe go? That question is answered very directly by God in Malachi 3. I've already established that the tithe is simple obedience, even in the New Testament. It follows that God didn't make any changes to His establishment of the tithe.

"'I the Lord do not change...Return to me, and I will return to you,' says the Lord Almighty. But you ask, 'How are we to return?' Will a mere mortal rob God? Yet you rob me. But you ask, 'How are we robbing you?'

*'In tithes and offerings. You are under a curse – your whole nation – because you are robbing me. **Bring the whole tithe into the storehouse**, that there may be food in **My house**. Test me in this,' says the Lord Almighty, 'and see if I will not throw open the floodgates of heaven and **pour out so much blessing that there will not be room enough to store it'.***"[27]

---

[27] Malachi 3:6-10

It's hard to make it any clearer. The tithe belongs to the storehouse. God's house, the church where you receive spiritual nourishment. It's the first priority. God tells the Israelites again in the book of Haggai that they've made His house a low priority. The consequences of not building God's house are shown in Haggai 1:4-11:

"Is it a time for you to be living in paneled houses, while this (God's) house remains a ruin? ...Give careful thought to your ways. You have planted much, but harvested little. You eat, but never have enough...You earn wages, only to put them in a purse with holes in it...Give careful thought to your ways...and build my house, so that I may take pleasure in it and be honored...You expected much, but see, it turned out to be little. What you brought home, I blew away. Because of my (God's) house, which remains a ruin, while each of you is busy with your own house. Therefore, because of you the heavens have withheld their dew...I called for a drought on the fields and the mountains...on people and livestock, and on all the labor of your hands."

Wow! God isn't playing around. His house is a priority. For the Christian today, that's the local church.

As we build God's house, He will build ours. Do we have faith to believe that God can bless our lives while we give away 10% to God? When we remove God's hand from our lives, our 100% is much less able to provide than the 90% He allows us to do.

While I was preaching overseas, I experienced a miracle that demonstrates the power of giving to God that which is – the tithe.

I was in a poor village in New Guinea and the people came up – they didn't have money – with a love offering for us. We were ministering during Easter week. They brought eggs, coconuts, and chickens. I told the pastor, "I don't want any of these offerings, I want it to go to you and the church."

The pastor told me that they gave every tenth chicken, egg, coconut, etc. to the church. The people were living blessed lives in their community because they were committed to the principle of tithing.

On our last day there, a coconut fell out of the tree and killed a chicken. The pastor said, "That chicken was a tithe. Be healed chicken, you belong to God!" The chicken jumped back up and started clucking as though nothing had happened!

You can trust God with the tithe. He will take care of His people. He even takes care of the chickens in New Guinea!

We give dues to all sorts of clubs and groups. God's dues are a tithe. I often tell people that our wallets are often the last thing to get saved. The first practical step for getting your harvest – and for living a life that prospers – is tithing.

Praise

Now that you understand the proper financial perspectives for living a life that prospers, I want to make one more point about how we relate to money.

Prosperity is not the accumulation of things.

Blessing is not what you have, it's what you have left after you've paid all your bills. Blessing is not living up to your neck in debt.

Maybe right now, you're in a bad spot. Maybe you don't financially have anywhere near what you want or even need.

The next step in a life that prospers is to give Praise, even when you don't feel like it. Especially when you don't feel like it.

The sacrifices offered to God in the Old Testament had to be the best. The sheep, doves, and other animals had to be flawless. They had to be premium, Grade-A quality. Thankfully, Jesus came and we no longer have to take an animal to a priest to be gutted on an altar. But, even though Jesus came, the New Testament mentions sacrifice still. To have a life that prospers, you need to be able to bring **a sacrifice of praise.**

"Through Jesus, therefore, let us continually offer to God a sacrifice of praise – the fruit of lips that openly profess His name."[28]

The sacrifice of praise is brought when we praise God during difficult times. Like Paul and Silas, who sang praises to God while chained in a dingy prison, we are to worship Him no matter what's happening in our life. And, like Paul and Silas, eventually, the chains will break. God can't resist responding to those who offer Him a sacrifice of praise.

The fruit of our lips is to give thanks. *Homologia* is the Greek word which means "to say the same words that God has said." Our lips are to offer

---

[28] Hebrews 13:15

words that agree with what God has said. Even when it doesn't look like God is anywhere to be found!

We are to declare our agreement with God. Not what life tells us, and not what our circumstances appear to be. Not what the stock market and the newscasters say. We speak through what God has to say.
When we praise Him, our attitude changes. When we bring a sacrifice of praise, we honor God and He in turn, responds to us.

The next time something bad happens in your life, try playing worship music – wherever you are – and praising God. Watch your spirit be lifted. Watch your faith be lifted. Watch God prosper you, in spite of the negative circumstances surrounding you. Sometimes in order to prosper – you need to **Praise.**

Blessed

What does it mean to be blessed? Lots of people have opinions. Everyone has a specific area that matters more to them than anything else. Rather than try to pinpoint what being blessed means to everyone, I'll stick with the dictionary definition.

Blessed means "happy, fortunate, to be envied."

The Bible tells us that blessed are they who fear the Lord. Blessed are those who surrender to Him and obey Him. Blessed are those who take responsibility. Blessed are those who repent. Blessed are those who endure. Blessed are those who give.

There ought to be something about your life that brings happiness to others. There ought to be evidence of blessing that attracts others to what God is doing in your life – and what you are doing in the lives of others because you are blessed.

The Bible says that there is fullness of joy, and strength in His presence.

One of my favorite examples of the blessing that comes from the presence of God is the story of a man called Obed-Edom. 2 Samuel 6 tells the story of this man, and he is also found in 1 Chronicles 13 & 16.

King David was transporting the Ark of the Covenant, the physical presence of God, with a group of men. As one man stumbled, the Ark began to fall to the ground. Another man reached out to catch the Ark, and he was killed by making contact with God's presence!

King David didn't know what to do. He didn't want anyone else to die. He was upset because the man was only trying to help. So, they carried the Ark (without touching it with their hands) into the house of a man who happened to live nearby. His name was Obed-Edom.

During the next three months, the Ark stayed in Obed-Edom's house, and "the Lord blessed him and his entire household."[29]

Because of the presence of God, Obed-Edom's entire family was blessed. It's no different today, in fact it's better. We can enter God's presence any time, all the time. All we have to do is praise Him.

Some Christians are constantly walking around weak and miserable. It makes me wonder if they've been in the presence of God.

Some people take a vow of poverty. I think it takes no faith to be poor. It's easy to be poor. But, this book is about more than money. Just as Jesus was.

I tell people all the time, Jesus wasn't poor. He would have refused to have a used car. When He sent the disciples in to get Him a ride, they got a new colt! Now, I'm being humorous, but I believe

---

[29] 2 Samuel 6:11 (NIV)

it. Jesus was not poor. Look at the gifts that were brought to him by the wise men!

When Jesus talked about being poor, he wasn't talking about being impoverished or depressed or weak. Some people have misquoted the Beatitudes. Jesus was talking about being totally dependent on God. He was talking about having an awareness that we need Him for everything.

Though Jesus was rich, he became poor so that through Him we might be made rich. He said, "I have come that you might have life more abundantly. The thief comes to steal and kill and destroy."[30]

Satan comes to make you impoverished. Jesus comes to bring abundance.

I promised some practical points for how to build a life that prospers. I've shared the necessity of

---

[30] John 10:10

tithing, and bringing praise. Here's another one –
Work hard.

Hard work is mentioned over and over again in the
Bible, especially the book of Proverbs. Check out
the verses listed below:

> Proverbs 10:15
> Proverbs 11:24
> Proverbs 13:18
> Proverbs 14:23
> Proverbs 20:13
> Proverbs 22:16
> Proverbs 23:21
> Proverbs 28:22

Take the time to read each of those verses in your
Bible. In case you want to do it later, here's a quick
summary of what they say:

*Word hard. Do not love sleep. Get up and go to
work. Live with discipline. Don't be a glutton, or a
drunkard. People without control over their
appetites end in poverty.*

Poverty is a work of the curse, and Jesus has come to bring us out of it. 2 Corinthians 8:9 says, *"For you know the grace of our Lord Jesus Christ...He became poor to break the curse of poverty."*

If you are ready for a harvest, here are five keys that I've found are absolutely crucial:

1. **Sow seeds** (give in a manner that is connected to what you anticipate receiving)

2. **Get in the right environment** (be involved in your local church. Be surrounded by an atmosphere of faith)

3. **Be patient** (don't dig up your seed – let it grow)

4. **Don't eat your seed** (2 Corinthians 9:10 – Now He who supplies seed to the sower and bread for food will also supply and increase your store of seed and will enlarge the harvest of your righteousness)

5. **Refuse giving fatigue** (Galatians 6:9 – Don't grow weary while doing good; in due season you'll reap if you don't faint)

I finish this book with a personal example. This is a true story and it's an example of what happens when you live by the principles in this book. I hope it encourages you to trust God and believe His promises for your life – to truly prosper – to live generous and to be blessed.

When I first became a youth pastor, I was working at a good job, with a sold income. I even had a company car! My pastor asked me to consider becoming the youth pastor. I accepted the pastor's invitation, not thinking about what I'd earn.

It was 1983. Sharon and I were newly married and were planning on saving for a house and to have kids. My net income before taking the youth pastor position was $400 a week.

After my first week as a youth pastor, I received my salary. The gross income was 33% of what I'd been making during my other job. I was now making $169 a week. Gross income! Our monthly rent was $110!

I didn't want to go home. When I finally got home, and told Sharon what I was now being paid, she was certainly displeased. I was mad at God. I told Him so, and I heard very clearly the Lord remind me "It's all according to my riches and glory." This was a turning point for me. I told Sharon and we resolved to trust God and not man for all that God has to provide for us.

A few weeks later, Sharon said that she was going to believe God for a house for $55,000. At the time, the cheapest house in any kind of safe neighborhood was $75,000. I told her she was ridiculous.

I believe I said, "I understand faith but that's just crazy, you know!"

The next day, Sharon saw an ad in the paper for a house for $56,000. It was a three-bedroom house on a ¼ acre of land. Sharon called right away and told the owner that we'd like to buy that house. As we were going to meet the man who was selling the house, I felt the Lord tell me to bring $200. I got $200 and put it in my wallet.

When we got to the meeting with the homeowner, he told us that multiple real estate agents had called offering $70,000. Then he said, "I don't trust realtors."

I told him, "Me neither." Hey, whatever he was saying, I was going to agree.

The older man said, "I like you two and I don't need $70,000 for this house. Because you're the first to call and a newly married couple, if you have $200 to put down, I'll sell the house to you for $56,000. We ended up buying that house for $56,000.

We sold that house one year later for $104,000!

Isn't that amazing! God is so good. How did that happen? Because God wants to bless us. It's not just a case of being in the right place at the right time. Sharon was praying and trusting God. We heard from Him and we followed His leading. When you have faith in God, your faith has the ability to attract and produce. Just as fear has the ability to produce and attract.

Fear is the substance of things dreaded.

Faith is the substance of things hoped for. Faith will bring the results you desire. Psalm 37:4 tells us, *"Take delight in the Lord and He will give you the desires of your heart."*

I believe it with all my heart. I've experienced it in my own life and I've seen it in the lives of many, many others.

You can prosper. The Lord is with you. Believe His word. Believe His promises. Take Responsibility. Choose Life. Be a friend of Jesus - be Obedient.

Listen to His word. Repent if necessary. Endure. Give.

I pray you take the message of this book to heart. I believe if you do, you will discover what it means to Prosper. And I know you will become Generous, and you – and your family – will live Blessed!

Made in the USA
Middletown, DE
16 July 2019